STEM CAREERS
BOTANIST

by R.J. Bailey

pogo

Ideas for Parents and Teachers

Pogo Books let children practice reading informational text while introducing them to nonfiction features such as headings, labels, sidebars, maps, and diagrams, as well as a table of contents, glossary, and index.

Carefully leveled text with a strong photo match offers early fluent readers the support they need to succeed.

Before Reading

- "Walk" through the book and point out the various nonfiction features. Ask the student what purpose each feature serves.
- Look at the glossary together. Read and discuss the words.

Read the Book

- Have the child read the book independently.
- Invite him or her to list questions that arise from reading.

After Reading

- Discuss the child's questions. Talk about how he or she might find answers to those questions.
- Prompt the child to think more. Ask: Do you know anyone who works as a botanist? What projects has he or she been involved in? Do you have any interest in this kind of work?

Pogo Books are published by Jump!
5357 Penn Avenue South
Minneapolis, MN 55419
www.jumplibrary.com

Library of Congress Cataloging-in-Publication Data

Names: Bailey, R.J., author.
Title: Botanist / by R.J. Bailey.
Description: Minneapolis, MN: Jump!, Inc., [2019]
Series: STEM careers | Audience: Age 7-10.
Includes index.
Identifiers: LCCN 2018014521 (print)
LCCN 2018017325 (ebook)
ISBN 9781641281775 (ebook)
ISBN 9781641281768 (hardcover: alk. paper)
Subjects: LCSH: Botanists–Juvenile literature.
Botany–Vocational guidance–Juvenile literature.
Classification: LCC QK50.5 (ebook)
LCC QK50.5 .B35 2019 (print) | DDC 580.92–dc23
LC record available at https://lccn.loc.gov/2018014521

Editors: Jenna Trnka and Susanne Bushman
Designer: Michelle Sonnek

Photo Credits: Kitch Bain/Shutterstock, cover; Blaj Gabriel/Shutterstock, 1; Levent Konuk/Shutterstock, 3; Anton-Burakov/Shutterstock, 4l; arka38/Shutterstock, 4r; Trong Nguyen/Shutterstock, 5; Budimir Jevtic/Shutterstock, 6-7; ARTFULLY PHOTOGRAPHER/Shutterstock, 8-9; Chutima Chaochaiya/Shutterstock, 10-11; DESCAMPS Simon/Hemis/Superstock, 12; Auscape/Getty, 13; De Visu/Shutterstock, 14-15 (background); web2000ra/Shutterstock, 14 (leaves); Jacek Fulawka/Shutterstock, 15 (trowel); LightField Studios/Shutterstock, 16-17; Paul Hakimata Photography/Shutterstock, 18; espies/Shutterstock, 19; Dragon Images/Shutterstock, 20-21; kkkawpunnn/Shutterstock, 23.

Printed in the United States of America at Corporate Graphics in North Mankato, Minnesota.

TABLE OF CONTENTS

CHAPTER 1

PLANT PEOPLE

People and animals need plants to live. Plants give us food to eat. They give us air to breathe. They form **habitats**, such as forests and grasslands. These natural areas provide homes for animals.

People use plants in other ways, too. How? To make useful things. Clothing. Building materials. Even **medicine**.

Botany is the study of plants. It is a branch of **biology**. Plants include flowers, trees, grasses, and seaweed. They include tiny plants that you need a microscope to see.

Scientists who study plants are called botanists. They study how plants grow. And what they are made up of. They also search for new **species**.

DID YOU KNOW?

There are about 400,000 plant species on Earth. Botanists continue to look for new plants. New plants may become important sources for food and medicine.

microscope

Botanists use what they learn to improve ways to grow food. They look for new sources of **fuel**. They also identify and remove materials from plants. These materials are used to make everyday objects, such as paper and makeup.

DID YOU KNOW?

Ethanol is a fuel. It is made from corn and sugar plants. We use it to power some cars.

Raising plants for human and animal food uses a lot of water. It uses a lot of **energy**. The chemicals farmers use to grow food can cause **pollution**. These things contribute to **climate change**. This can lead to **drought**. This hurts plant growth. Botanists explore ways to grow plants that can survive during droughts.

CHAPTER 2

WHAT DO THEY DO?

Botanists work in different settings. Some work outside. Or in **greenhouses**. This is called working in the field.

They work in different **climates**.
Like what? Deserts and rain forests.
Some even work underwater!

magnifying glass

In the field, botanists use magnifying glasses to see plants up close. They use **trowels** to collect plant samples. They use plant presses to save samples. They use cameras to document plant species. They write notes.

trowel

Other botanists spend time in the lab. They use microscopes to look at tiny plant samples. They use computers to look up information about plants. Other botanists have gathered this information over time.

TAKE A LOOK!

Botanists use microscopes. These help them see things invisible to the unaided eye.

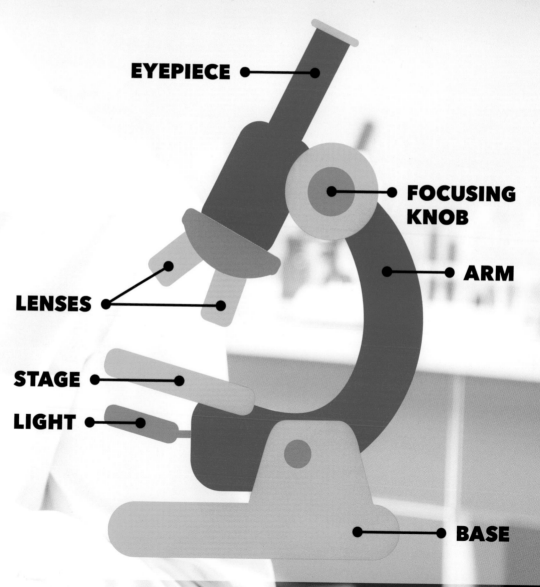

EYEPIECE

FOCUSING KNOB

ARM

LENSES

STAGE

LIGHT

BASE

CHAPTER 3

BECOMING A BOTANIST

Are you comfortable outdoors? Do you like to camp? Are you curious about the plants you see? You could be a botanist!

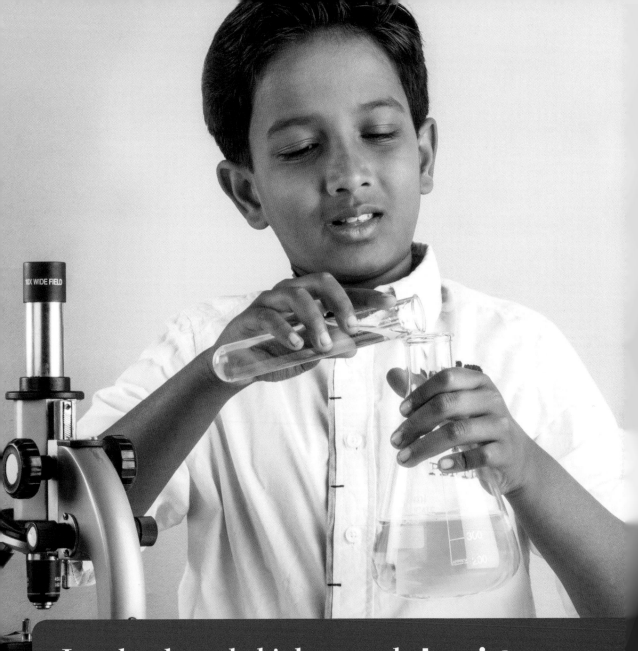

In school, study biology and **chemistry**. Study math and history. Join a science club. You will also need computer skills. Plan to spend at least four years in college.

As a botanist, you can shape the future. How? You could find new ways to feed more people. You could end a disease. You could discover a new fuel. What would you like to do as a botanist?

DID YOU KNOW?

To work as a botanist, you need STEM skills. What does STEM stand for? Science. Technology. Engineering. Math. STEM careers are in demand. They pay well, too.

ACTIVITIES & TOOLS

TRY THIS!

PRESSING FLOWERS

Botanists press flowers and other plants so they can save them to study later. Press and study your own flowers!

What You Need:
- freshly-picked flowers
- sheet of newspaper or waxed paper
- large, heavy book
- more books or heavy objects
- notebook
- pencil

1. Pick fresh flowers. Put them inside a folded sheet of newspaper or wax paper. Make sure there are no overlapping leaves, petals, or stems.

2. Open the large, heavy book. Put the folded paper in the middle of it. Close the book. Put other books or heavy objects on top of it.

3. Wait three days for the flowers to dry. Open the book and study the flowers. What do you see? Document your findings.

4. After you are done studying your pressed plants, you can put them in flower arrangements, give them as gifts, or use them in crafts or artwork.

biology: The study of life and living things.

chemistry: A science that deals with the structure of substances and the changes that they go through.

climate change: A change in global or regional climate patterns that are linked to the burning of fuels, such as oil, natural gas, and coal.

climates: The common weather conditions of particular areas over a period of time.

drought: A long period without rain.

energy: The ability to do work.

fuel: Something that is used as a source of heat or energy, such as coal, wood, gasoline, or natural gas.

greenhouses: Enclosed structures for plants that have controlled lighting and heat so that the plants inside can grow even when it is cold.

habitats: Places where animals and plants live and grow.

medicine: Substances, such as drugs, that are used to treat illnesses.

pollution: Harmful substances that damage or contaminate the air, water, or soil.

species: A grouping of things of the same kind and with the same name that are able to reproduce to create fertile offspring.

trowels: Small hand tools with curved blades that are used for digging.

INDEX

TO LEARN MORE

Finding more information is as easy as 1, 2, 3.

1 **Go to www.factsurfer.com**

2 **Enter "botanist" into the search box.**

3 **Click the "Surf" button to see a list of websites.**

FACT SURFER